Riding on a Seahorse

ROSHAN B. KARKI

ISBN: 9798828176892

DEDICATION

To my Wife Roshina

CONTENTS

ACKNOWLEDGMENTS

POEMS ABOUT MYTHICAL SUBJECTS

Like a Spiderman

I cannot fight with spider wasps.
Nor can I fly like a bat.
But if the world needs me;
if you need me as a friend
Just call my name
Like a Spiderman- I will come

I am with truth, freedom and justice.
I do not cast shadows like tall trees.
If you need me as friend
just call my name
Like a Spiderman- I will come

Riding a Sea Horse

Once I rode a sea horse
Deep in Sea
to meet sea god.

Its saddle was golden.
It was faster than
anything in the world.
It took me to sea God.

The nymphs his guards
praised me and my love.
I made a request to meet sea god.

The sea god said,
"Welcome friend.
Here in sea bed.
We do not let humans
live with us.
If you want to live with us
you must be fishes first."

So he changed me into a God
and my lover to a mermaid.

That's how mermaid came to existence in this world.

Sinbad the Sailor

Row on the sea
like Sinbad the sailor
Search for wealth
and head for adventures
in any weather.

The seven voyages
were all like a miracle.
Home he brought the treasures
each journey he found something better

Now he rests in palaces
with beautiful women and followers.
He recites his stories
of his adventures.

Life is a sea
You are a boat
Search for treasures
in any weathers

Calm is the sea
Yours in the world
Row down the boat
Like Sinbad the Sailor

The Civilizations

There was Atlantis.
There was Lemuria.
Here is Nepal
and here is America.

The civilizations were not made by God alone.
It was made by people, their beliefs and gratitude.

The Mayans had pyramids
we have satellites.
I wonder what our next civilizations will be like.

The civilizations are not made alone by Gods.

The Dragons are real

Once I witnessed a dragon
breathing fire up high in the sky.
It was flying with bat like wings.
I do not know till now
whether it was real or dreams.

I breathe air
He breathes fire
Clap for the amazing dragon

It came to my place
and burned the stones.
If it could fly up high
it would have burned the moon.

--------------------*******************----------------

The dragon in my dreams
haunted me.
Can I fly up in the sky?
It wondered me.

I made wings
with feathers and leaves.
I went up in the cliff, put the wings
and jumped from it.

Now I am in Lord's Kingdom.
There are dragons, mermaids and unicorns.

If it exists in your mind;
it must exist somewhere.

If you think they are,
the dragons are real.

Witnessed a Snow Man

I have witnessed a snow man.
It looked as if it was member of some clan.
He looked to me as if I was mysterious.
I looked at him with wonder.

He was dressed in white feathers.
I was dressed in a jacket made of leathers.
It was so cold. He offered me ride
to his home. He took out a kettle.

He offered me tea. He offered me milk.
Then he fed his children.
I felt warm. I felt better.
I felt the myths were real.

I stayed with him a month and a day.
Every day was beautiful like Christmas day.
He took me to underground tunnels in snow.
He took me places where treasures laid.

Soon it was time to say good bye.
He said bye-bye with tear in his eye.
We have bonded like brothers.
Our love could have gathered a number of followers.

What are the people doing
with hate and anger?
Learn something from snowman.
He treated a human being like a brother.

POEMS ABOUT MY WIFE ROSHINA

A Cup of Tea

Welcome me in the mornings with cup of tea.
I like a lot of sugar in my tea like a bee.
Your beauty shimmers in sun rays.
We will drink tea in the morning to start our day.

The day will be busy but we will remember each
other.
Here love is a bill we will both fulfill.
Each day I am grateful to you.
Welcome me in the mornings with cup of tea.

As I sip tea like a bee.
I feel I am kissing your lips.
We have whole life to live.
Welcome me in the morning with cup of tea.

A Love Letter to Roshina

I am no good at writing love letters.
The moon is in sky
and I am in my room with feelings.
The words are bold but I feel shy.

May your soul find me as lover?
Your beauty is like sunflowers
the God planted in this earth
to be together forever.

May your lips kiss me?
Let me feel beautiful
in this life and hundreds of others.
This is my blood written feeling
I wrote in my heart as a love letter.

May you never feel lonely
I wish we will be together for the rest of life
Read it
Approve it
Feel it
We will be together
This life and hundreds of others.

This is my feelings to you as love letter.

As the Night Unfolds

Slowly like petals of flowers
the night unfolds.
And I feel I am a bee
to see the diving fragrance.

You smell of faint jasmine.
Today I will take you places
You have never been
And you have never
dared to imagine.
I will take you away from the world
to moons and constellations and
to Himalayas past time.

Let me feel you feel like feathers
as if it some kind of tether.
We are made for each other.

Soon it will be night and
the moon will be on sky.
Let you be my world tonight
and thousands of other
as the night unfolds
like petals of flowers.

Deepest Layer of Heaven

The angels play guitar
and sing about your beauty
In the deepest layer of heaven.
Here is eternity
here is love
here is luxury

Let the angels
hover around you and praise your beauty.
We are happy
in the deepest layer of heaven
created by love on earth.

For the First Lady

I am the president
Roshina, you are the first lady
The world is talking our talks
We are something like Royals already.

Let us sow the earth
With development, affection and love
I am the president and you are the first lady.
Let us cheer and make merry.

Let our family
be a model to others in the country.
Because these are our days
we are royals already.

Stared in your Eyes

I stared in your eyes.
Slowly the mystery of creation unfolded.
At first there was void and God created love.
Then he created you and me
He placed us on earth where heaven lie.
He gave us lips to kiss and mouth to drink wine.
He made days to wonder and nights to make love.
He created rain and thunder so that we can be
together.

This is how god created our world.

In his Image

No wonder why you are so beautiful
No wonder why you are so playful
The angels may envy your beauty
Because God created you in his image

No wonder why the moon shines for you
No wonder why painters paint your portrait
you are most beautiful. I bet.
It's because God created you in his image.

So you use your beauty. Let me kiss you.
Every day is vacation. Every day is new.
There are people who admire your beauty.
I am the one. Cause God created you in his image.

God created you as beautiful as the roses are.

In your Eyes

As I look in your eyes
I see constellations and skies.
I see beauty of distant sailors and seas.
I feel calmness of soft breeze passing by in trees.

As I look in your eyes
I bow down in my knees.
I surrender to your beauty.
You will be beautiful to me till eighties.

I dream of your dreams
you are so magical
like the moon in distant skies.
We will be together for thousands of lives.

My Girl

Your hair is beautiful
and you comb it too much
Let us share our talks
sipping fine wine.

You are a princess
and I am a prince.
One palace lies in our house.
The other lies in our hearts.

Let us talk and make merry.
The clock has stroke half past nine already.
Let we be together throughout the night.
We will go gentle tonight.

The god from heaven will
appear on sky tonight.
But we will be inside our huts
with our affection
with our love

Love must be something very shy.

Ode to Roshina

Your Aries charm
like a fire
Keeps me warm.
I dwell in your beauty.
We will be together till eighty.
We will be together till eternity.
Our love is almighty
we will live our life
with love and telepathy.

You make me wonder
in any seasons or in thunder.
My love I surrender
to your Aries charm.
I am a Libra man.
We are perfect couples.

You lips and words
Keeps me entertained.
As I kiss your lips
I feel I am under
Your spell of love .
We will be together
Until end of life
And hundreds more to come.
This is my ode to your Roshina.

Omnipresent Love

God should have seen you and me
and our affection for each other.
He must have seen my feelings for her.
Let us always be together, my omnipresent love.

I ask for nothing more.
Some bread and some wine.
A house and some luxuries
A fire and a secure future
Let us always be always together.
Oh! My omnipresent love.

Part of your Life

Like the sun is there for moon
you have become part of your life.
I am so blessed. I feel so delight
as we are together throughout the life.

Every day we will grow young together
with flowers, wine and feelings.
But the days are blessings and lessening
in the voyage of our life.

Even time won't affect our love.
The nymphs bless highly from sea bed.
Are we growing young or old? I wonder.
Thus to the power of love we surrender.

Roshina, as we Grow Old together

Roshina, as we grow old together
there will be more white then pink.
Scars will conquer us
but we will be almighty lovers of soul.

Will the seas look more beautiful?
Will the nymphs sing about our love?
I do not know. I will not know.
But there will be more white then pink and other
colors.

So let the walls fall down
and we will be together holding our hands.
But before we will get old
we will be almighty lovers of the soul.

Roshina, I Surrender to my Life to You

I know how it feels to surrender
your life to woman you love.
It feels heavenly as
if she is gifted by Gods.
Every inch of soul
feels you are connected to
every inch of her. The memories re create.
Time changes but love remains the same.
You dwell in your kingdom of love
free open and wild
Like wildflowers in rain.
It hurts your heart;
it traumatizes your soul if she is in pain.
The kiss and touch feels almighty
every night when you dwell
In free kingdom of love.
Let God bless us from heights.
Let painters paint our love in red
as red are the roses.
My woman, my friend, my lover
Roshina, I surrender my life to you

Roshina, Our palace

We are rich yet modest.
We are not planning for better;
we are aiming for the best.
We will not be afraid if Lord takes our test.
Roshina, our palace lies deep in our heart.

This Room

As I swim in your beauty
I deep in seas
I travel through constellations
I ride highest mountains

Your lips
Like the seas
Wide and wild
Thirsty for love

Your breasts
Like almighty Himalayas
Waiting to be conquered

Your skin
Soft and sensual
Waiting for a touch

Whose it this room
I think I know
You and me
We have made love here before.

Vows with Roshina

Since the day we took our vows
Loathing to be together for this life
And thousands of others
I feel I am a lucky person.

 Everyday your charm
Ignites my day
and lights up the lamp
Where I can see way to success.

You have changed me
but we still are the same.
It's been three years
there will be thousands of other.

Let lord bless our life
and bless with abundance.
We will make a perfect couple.
We will make a perfect couple.

What use are the Lips?

What use are the lips?
If they cannot kiss you
once in a long day
Your lips like a miracle
Keeps boring day away

What use are the lips?
If they cannot talk,
mutter and complain
about your beauty.
You are so beautiful.

What use the lips?
If little red of your lipstick
won't imprint on my lips
and feel I am you.

Your lips are so sensual.

POEMS ABOUT LIFE, TRAVELLING AND OTHER SUBJECTS

A Game of Card

The table is polished
and it is sparkling like diamonds.
There is no friendship here
when a deck of card is on table.

Shuffle it
Divide it
Fulfill it
That's what the King wants.

The ace is alone
and it is sign of victory.
The more are the aces
more is the money.

The dollars cheap
Lies on table
If I win it,
it is not me
It is the cards on the table.

A Sky full of Stars

If you look at the sky at night
you will see star.
Dream to be a one.
Let people talk about in bars.

Look at the sky full of stars.
Look how beautiful you are.
You can be the one
if you work hard.

As the Rain Drizzles

As the rain drizzles
it wipes down your black eye linings
and falls as tears
on the floor.

As the rain drizzles
It wets the red roses
In my garden of heart
and taller it grows.

As the rain drizzles
we walk under umbrella
as pair of lovers
wet in this world.

As the Way Diverged

You and I were together
when the way diverged.
You took a different path.
I took the next one.

We are deep in our lives.
Will we meet again?
I wish. I wonder.
The path is full of snow and thunder.

It's been years
we and I are far from each other.
But there are footprints
which are proofs we have walked together.

Some day if the fate will find us
the ways will meet
and we will be happily ever after.
But I doubt that.

Cycle Continues

Day unfolds
The moon appears
The sun goes down
History repeats
People walk
Tigers hunt
Preacher's pray
Beggar's beg

The cycle continues

Different Worlds

Everything you see in your eyes might not be true.
There are black, brown and white figures in the zoo.
So what is there to hurry, let us make merry.
Listen to Beethoven's sonata, read out stories.

Only love and humanity can brighten the world.
I will take you place you never had been told.
I will take you to palace and garden in my heart.
There can be new world and for it let us make a start.

There are ten decades and this can be a key to
eternity.
Let the world be full of joy. Let there be beauty.
Cause everything you see might not be true.
Everyone has a different world and so do you.

Let the Bell Chime

Let the bell chime
and party begin.
We have one life to live.
We won't get a chance to start again.

Let the bell chime
and you open the fine champagne
Let it feel the glasses like rain
and I will drink it
Cheering it to your name.

Let the bell chime
anytime in summer or spring.
Winter is too cold for us
It will freeze
Love and lovers.
I drink this glass of wine
cheering it to your name.

Life

Life can be full of ways, mazes and thunder.
There are stars in sky which make us wonder.
To the creator in some unknown place we surrender.
You and I can be close like brothers.

Here is youth and there is old age.
Some become preachers. Some become sage.
Between heaven and hell this world lays.
Here are ants and there are bells.

Study. Make money. Make love.
The life is not that bad at all.
But sometimes while trying
there will be failure

So ring the bells and make merry.
The sea is the world and you are a ferry.
Let the world tell tales about you.
There are proofs of people with magnificent lives
already.

Let the life and love bless you.
Let the life laden you with gold and wealth.
Come and say hello to each other.
Feel good and move further.

Say Hello

Why are you hurrying my friend?
The streets are busy yet silent.
Look at me and say hello
as you pass by.

There is a lot to win
and there are few things to lose.
We both have won and lost.
Pass your hands and say hello.

You are a stranger. So am I.
I will shake hands with so do not feel shy.
Why are you hurrying my friend?
Look at my eyes and say hello.

The Other Worlds

Did you hear the bell chime
coming back to this world
with a speed of sound?
Is anyone there?
I am thinking about the other worlds.

What do you eat?
What do you wear?
Are you looking for a friend just like me?
I am thinking about the other worlds.

But you are enigmatic
as you do not let us know
you exist anywhere.
Hello! Can you hear me?
I am thinking about the other worlds.

Welcome You

Hey stranger
I want to welcome you
The city is full of talks
I welcome you to my huts.

Here the bread is brown
and soup is delicious.
It is pleasant in my hut
though it is made of clay and mud.

Sip some broth
and tell your stories
as you look like a warrior.
We are in both wars with life.

Slowly the midnight is here.
The dragons will be on sky.
But we will be safe and sound inside our huts.

Who Created Love?

Who created love?
Day by day
We are growing old
but our love
like a bottle of wine
gets better.
Love is only truth here
so fulfill it like a bill.

As we grow old together
in this ride
I feel I am more human.
Love will guide us.

But who created love
humans or gods?
Whoever it is
it has sustained the world.

POEMS ABOUT ME

All Alone my Life

I have been all alone my life
like the moon in distant skies.
Yet there were people and passersby
who wanted to talk with me in cold nights.

I have all alone my life
until I found you with beauty in your eyes.
I bet. I do not deal in lies
we will together till end of time.

I have been all alone my life
looking at the dark sky.
You came me to like a moon
and sowed my life with love and light.

I am Invincible

Throw down the problems of this world at my door.
It does not matter if I am young and old.
I will do things you never have been told.
I have been breaking barriers, commanding U.S
troops since six.
Now I am the president and I can solve famine and
poverty.
I am invincible. I can change the world.

42

My Whitehouse, My home

Thank the lord
I was born with certain qualities and gifts
and I am using it for a better world.
Roshina, the first lady is with me.
A man always not really needs towers and palaces
to fulfill his duties, to fulfill his bills.
Thank u all for your belief in me.
I think of people and paradise.
A great leader is what world needs
and I am trying to be the one.
I want to alleviate poverty, hunger
Lord let me fulfill my bills.
Cause now Whitehouse is my home.

Retired Colonel of Navy

The load was heavy.
We are half a century already.
We are retired colonel of the Navy
and for it we should feel lucky.

We have already lived
for God and heroism.
Now we will live another life
as you pass by sharing our stories.

Switch to Politics

Mama, you wanted me to be an engineer.
I felt a good school charge a lot of fair.
I want to do something good to the world.
I feel I can be the President of United States.
For it I will switch to politics.

Thank you all for my life

Whitehouse is my home
and I have a beautiful wife.
I am living a fairytale.
Thank you all for my life.

I could have never made it
without your support
and I will fulfill my bills
with my hard earned notes.

I vow to fulfill my duties.
I promised to continue it till my eighties.
Thank you! Thank you! Thank you!
Thank you all for my life.

Art of Winning

I know the art of winning as
throughout my life I have mostly won.
First comes with the desire.
A burning desire to win

The second is work.
Work hard on your crafts.
You ignore the critics.
You ignore the laughs.

The third is belief.
A strong belief for who you are.
If you do not have one
drink some liquor in a bar
it will come to you.

The next is some style.
Have some originality and style.
But sometimes the wheels will spin
and you may face dirt.

Now you will win and
always keep on wining

BONUS SHORT POEMS

Bonfire

Feel the fire
with champagne
we make bonfire once again

Prometheus

A Greek god
Stole fire and gave birth
to a human world

Poverty and Poetry

Some day poetry is art of poverty.
I deny it. I say no.
I do know a little bit of poetry
and I write it in effect of wine and whiskey.

I travel to places to places far and wide;
to be with nature, to be with god.
And I write lines
thinking about angel and their beauties.

To write poems fluently it takes time.
You have a job. Poetry is next one.
Until there is heartbeat; there will be poverty

ABOUT THE AUTHOR

Roshan B. Karki (Roshan Bikram Kark) is a poet, writer, musician and entrepreneur. He was born in Charikot, Dolkha. He has attended Loras College, USA as a honors student to pursue undergraduate in Creative writing. " Riding on a Seahorse" is fifteenth book by the author. It consists of poems about mythical subjects, love and life. These poems will entertain you like nothing else.

www.ingramcontent.com/pod-product-compliance
Lightning Source LLC
Chambersburg PA
CBHW060916130726
48001CB00006B/2271